50 Healthy Breakfast Recipes for Home

By: Kelly Johnson

Table of Contents

- Quinoa Stuffed Bell Peppers
- Grilled Salmon with Avocado Salsa
- Zucchini Noodles with Pesto
- Chicken and Vegetable Stir-Fry
- Baked Sweet Potato with Black Beans
- Spaghetti Squash with Tomato Basil Sauce
- Turkey and Spinach Meatballs
- Lentil and Vegetable Soup
- Cauliflower Fried Rice
- Greek Chicken Salad
- Baked Cod with Lemon and Herbs
- Chickpea and Spinach Curry
- Shrimp and Broccoli Skewers
- Stuffed Acorn Squash
- Teriyaki Chicken and Veggie Bowl
- Spicy Black Bean Tacos
- Grilled Portobello Mushrooms with Quinoa
- Mediterranean Quinoa Salad
- Baked Chicken Parmesan
- Roasted Vegetable and Hummus Wrap
- Miso Glazed Eggplant
- Turkey and Sweet Potato Chili
- Spinach and Feta Stuffed Chicken Breast
- Butternut Squash Risotto
- Thai Peanut Chicken Lettuce Wraps
- Roasted Salmon with Asparagus
- Chickpea and Kale Stew
- Greek Yogurt Chicken Salad
- Spaghetti with Butternut Squash Sauce
- Blackened Tilapia with Mango Salsa
- Zucchini and Tomato Frittata
- Beef and Broccoli Stir-Fry

- Cauliflower and Chickpea Tacos
- Quinoa and Roasted Vegetable Bowl
- Pesto Chicken and Veggie Skewers
- Creamy Avocado Pasta
- Stuffed Zucchini Boats
- Lemon Garlic Shrimp with Spinach
- Beef and Sweet Potato Hash
- Moroccan Spiced Chickpeas
- Baked Tilapia with Sweet Potatoes
- Lentil and Sweet Potato Shepherd's Pie
- Roasted Brussels Sprouts with Garlic and Lemon
- Sweet Potato and Black Bean Enchiladas
- Chicken and Mushroom Stir-Fry
- Mediterranean Stuffed Eggplant
- Teriyaki Tofu and Vegetable Stir-Fry
- Grilled Chicken with Roasted Red Pepper Sauce
- Spaghetti Squash with Puttanesca Sauce
- Creamy Coconut Curry with Cauliflower

Quinoa Stuffed Bell Peppers

Ingredients:

- 4 large bell peppers (any color)
- 1 cup quinoa
- 2 cups vegetable broth (or water)
- 1 cup black beans, drained and rinsed
- 1 cup corn kernels (fresh, frozen, or canned)
- 1 cup cherry tomatoes, halved
- 1/2 cup red onion, finely chopped
- 1 cup shredded cheese (cheddar, Monterey Jack, or a dairy-free alternative)
- 1 teaspoon ground cumin
- 1 teaspoon paprika
- 1/2 teaspoon garlic powder
- Salt and pepper to taste
- 2 tablespoons olive oil
- Fresh cilantro or parsley for garnish (optional)

Instructions:

1. **Preheat Oven:**
   - Preheat your oven to 375°F (190°C).
2. **Prepare Quinoa:**
   - Rinse the quinoa under cold water. In a medium saucepan, bring the vegetable broth (or water) to a boil. Add the quinoa, reduce heat to low, cover, and simmer for about 15 minutes, or until the quinoa is cooked and the liquid is absorbed. Fluff with a fork and set aside.
3. **Prepare Bell Peppers:**
   - Cut the tops off the bell peppers and remove the seeds and membranes. If needed, trim the bottom slightly to help the peppers stand upright, but be careful not to cut through.
4. **Mix Filling:**
   - In a large bowl, combine the cooked quinoa, black beans, corn, cherry tomatoes, red onion, shredded cheese, cumin, paprika, garlic powder, salt, and pepper. Mix well to combine.
5. **Stuff Peppers:**
   - Place the bell peppers in a baking dish. Drizzle a little olive oil over the peppers. Spoon the quinoa mixture into each bell pepper, packing it in gently.
6. **Bake:**
   - Cover the baking dish with aluminum foil and bake in the preheated oven for 25-30 minutes. Remove the foil and bake for an additional 5-10 minutes, or until the peppers are tender and the filling is heated through.

7. **Garnish and Serve:**
    - Remove from the oven and let cool slightly. Garnish with fresh cilantro or parsley if desired. Serve warm.

Enjoy your healthy and flavorful quinoa-stuffed bell peppers!

Grilled Salmon with Avocado Salsa

Ingredients:

For the Salmon:

- 4 salmon fillets (6 oz each)
- 2 tablespoons olive oil
- 1 tablespoon lemon juice
- 1 teaspoon garlic powder
- 1 teaspoon paprika
- 1 teaspoon dried oregano
- Salt and pepper to taste

For the Avocado Salsa:

- 2 ripe avocados, diced
- 1 cup cherry tomatoes, halved
- 1/4 cup red onion, finely chopped
- 2 tablespoons fresh cilantro, chopped
- 1 tablespoon lime juice
- Salt and pepper to taste

Instructions:

1. **Prepare the Marinade:**
   - In a small bowl, mix together olive oil, lemon juice, garlic powder, paprika, dried oregano, salt, and pepper.
2. **Marinate the Salmon:**
   - Brush the salmon fillets with the marinade. Let them marinate for at least 15 minutes, or up to 1 hour in the refrigerator for more flavor.
3. **Prepare the Avocado Salsa:**
   - In a medium bowl, combine diced avocados, cherry tomatoes, red onion, and cilantro. Add lime juice, salt, and pepper to taste. Mix gently to combine. Set aside.
4. **Preheat the Grill:**
   - Preheat your grill to medium-high heat. If using a grill pan, preheat it over medium-high heat on the stovetop.
5. **Grill the Salmon:**
   - Place the salmon fillets skin-side down on the grill. Cook for about 4-5 minutes per side, or until the salmon is opaque and flakes easily with a fork. The exact time will depend on the thickness of the fillets.
6. **Serve:**

- Remove the salmon from the grill and let it rest for a few minutes. Top each fillet with a generous amount of avocado salsa.
7. **Enjoy:**
   - Serve the grilled salmon with avocado salsa immediately.

This dish pairs well with a side of steamed vegetables or a fresh green salad. Enjoy your healthy and delicious meal!

Zucchini Noodles with Pesto

Ingredients:

For the Zucchini Noodles:

- 4 medium zucchinis
- 1 tablespoon olive oil
- Salt and pepper to taste

For the Pesto:

- 2 cups fresh basil leaves
- 1/2 cup pine nuts (or walnuts)
- 1/2 cup grated Parmesan cheese (or a dairy-free alternative)
- 2 cloves garlic
- 1/2 cup olive oil
- Juice of 1/2 lemon
- Salt and pepper to taste

Optional Garnishes:

- Cherry tomatoes, halved
- Extra grated Parmesan cheese
- Fresh basil leaves

Instructions:

1. **Prepare Zucchini Noodles:**
   - Use a spiralizer to cut the zucchinis into noodles. Alternatively, you can use a julienne peeler or a mandoline with a julienne blade.
   - Place the zucchini noodles in a colander, sprinkle with a little salt, and let them sit for about 10 minutes to draw out excess moisture. Pat dry with paper towels.
2. **Make the Pesto:**
   - In a food processor or blender, combine basil leaves, pine nuts, Parmesan cheese, and garlic. Pulse until finely chopped.
   - With the processor running, slowly stream in the olive oil until the pesto reaches your desired consistency. You might need a bit more or less oil, so add it gradually.
   - Add lemon juice, salt, and pepper. Blend again until well combined. Taste and adjust seasoning if needed.
3. **Cook the Zucchini Noodles:**
   - Heat olive oil in a large skillet over medium heat.

- Add the zucchini noodles and cook for about 2-3 minutes, stirring frequently, until they are slightly tender but still crisp. Avoid overcooking to prevent them from becoming mushy.
- Season with a little salt and pepper.
4. **Combine:**
    - Remove the skillet from heat. Add the pesto to the zucchini noodles and toss to coat evenly.
5. **Serve:**
    - Serve immediately, topped with optional garnishes like halved cherry tomatoes, extra Parmesan cheese, and fresh basil leaves if desired.

Enjoy your light and flavorful zucchini noodles with pesto!

Chicken and Vegetable Stir-Fry

Ingredients:

For the Stir-Fry:

- 1 lb (450 g) boneless, skinless chicken breasts or thighs, thinly sliced
- 2 tablespoons olive oil or sesame oil
- 1 red bell pepper, sliced
- 1 yellow bell pepper, sliced
- 1 cup broccoli florets
- 1 cup snap peas or green beans
- 1 medium carrot, sliced thinly
- 1 cup mushrooms, sliced
- 2 cloves garlic, minced
- 1 tablespoon fresh ginger, minced (or 1 teaspoon ground ginger)
- 2 green onions, sliced

For the Sauce:

- 1/4 cup low-sodium soy sauce or tamari
- 2 tablespoons hoisin sauce
- 1 tablespoon rice vinegar
- 1 tablespoon honey or maple syrup
- 1 teaspoon cornstarch mixed with 1 tablespoon water (optional, for thickening)

Instructions:

1. **Prepare the Sauce:**
   - In a small bowl, whisk together the soy sauce, hoisin sauce, rice vinegar, and honey (or maple syrup). Set aside.
2. **Cook the Chicken:**
   - Heat 1 tablespoon of oil in a large skillet or wok over medium-high heat. Add the sliced chicken and cook, stirring frequently, until cooked through and lightly browned, about 5-7 minutes. Remove the chicken from the skillet and set aside.
3. **Stir-Fry the Vegetables:**
   - In the same skillet, add the remaining tablespoon of oil. Add the garlic and ginger, and cook for about 30 seconds until fragrant.
   - Add the bell peppers, broccoli, snap peas, carrots, and mushrooms. Stir-fry for 4-5 minutes, or until the vegetables are tender-crisp.
4. **Combine Everything:**
   - Return the cooked chicken to the skillet with the vegetables. Pour the sauce over the chicken and vegetables. Stir well to coat everything evenly. If you prefer a

thicker sauce, stir in the cornstarch mixture and cook for an additional minute or until the sauce has thickened.
5. **Finish and Serve:**
    - Stir in the green onions. Taste and adjust seasoning if needed.
    - Serve hot, over steamed rice, quinoa, or noodles if desired.

Enjoy your flavorful and healthy Chicken and Vegetable Stir-Fry!

Baked Sweet Potato with Black Beans

Ingredients:

For the Sweet Potatoes:

- 4 medium sweet potatoes
- 1 tablespoon olive oil
- Salt and pepper to taste

For the Black Beans:

- 1 can (15 oz) black beans, drained and rinsed
- 1/2 cup corn kernels (fresh, frozen, or canned)
- 1/2 cup cherry tomatoes, halved
- 1/4 cup red onion, finely chopped
- 1/2 teaspoon ground cumin
- 1/2 teaspoon chili powder
- 1/4 teaspoon garlic powder
- 1 tablespoon lime juice
- Salt and pepper to taste

Optional Toppings:

- Fresh cilantro, chopped
- Sliced avocado
- Crumbled feta cheese or shredded cheese
- Greek yogurt or sour cream

Instructions:

1. **Preheat Oven:**
    - Preheat your oven to 400°F (200°C).
2. **Prepare Sweet Potatoes:**
    - Wash and scrub the sweet potatoes. Pat them dry.
    - Pierce each sweet potato a few times with a fork. Rub with olive oil and season with salt and pepper.
    - Place the sweet potatoes on a baking sheet and bake for 40-50 minutes, or until they are tender and easily pierced with a fork. The exact time will depend on the size of the sweet potatoes.
3. **Prepare the Black Beans:**
    - In a medium bowl, combine the black beans, corn, cherry tomatoes, red onion, cumin, chili powder, garlic powder, lime juice, salt, and pepper. Mix well.
4. **Assemble:**

        ○ Once the sweet potatoes are done, remove them from the oven and let them cool slightly.
        ○ Cut each sweet potato down the center and gently fluff the flesh with a fork.
 5. **Top and Serve:**
        ○ Spoon the black bean mixture over the sweet potatoes.
        ○ Add any optional toppings such as fresh cilantro, avocado slices, crumbled feta cheese, or a dollop of Greek yogurt.

Enjoy your delicious and hearty Baked Sweet Potato with Black Beans!

Spaghetti Squash with Tomato Basil Sauce

Ingredients:

For the Spaghetti Squash:

- 1 large spaghetti squash
- 1 tablespoon olive oil
- Salt and pepper to taste

For the Tomato Basil Sauce:

- 1 tablespoon olive oil
- 1 medium onion, finely chopped
- 2 cloves garlic, minced
- 1 can (14.5 oz) crushed tomatoes
- 1/4 cup tomato paste
- 1 teaspoon dried basil
- 1/2 teaspoon dried oregano
- 1/4 teaspoon red pepper flakes (optional, for heat)
- Salt and pepper to taste
- 1/4 cup fresh basil leaves, chopped

Optional Toppings:

- Grated Parmesan cheese or a dairy-free alternative
- Fresh basil leaves

Instructions:

1. **Prepare the Spaghetti Squash:**
   - Preheat your oven to 400°F (200°C).
   - Cut the spaghetti squash in half lengthwise and scoop out the seeds. Drizzle the cut sides with olive oil and season with salt and pepper.
   - Place the squash halves cut-side down on a baking sheet lined with parchment paper or foil.
   - Bake for 40-45 minutes, or until the squash is tender and the strands can be easily shredded with a fork. The baking time may vary depending on the size of the squash.
2. **Make the Tomato Basil Sauce:**
   - While the squash is baking, heat olive oil in a medium saucepan over medium heat.
   - Add the chopped onion and cook until softened and translucent, about 5 minutes.
   - Add the minced garlic and cook for an additional 30 seconds until fragrant.

- Stir in the crushed tomatoes, tomato paste, dried basil, dried oregano, and red pepper flakes (if using). Simmer the sauce for about 10-15 minutes, allowing the flavors to meld. Season with salt and pepper to taste.
- Stir in the fresh basil leaves just before serving.
3. **Assemble the Dish:**
    - Once the spaghetti squash is done baking, use a fork to scrape out the flesh into strands.
    - Place the squash strands in a serving bowl or plate. Top with the warm tomato basil sauce.
4. **Serve:**
    - Garnish with optional toppings like grated Parmesan cheese or additional fresh basil leaves if desired.
    - Serve warm and enjoy your healthy and flavorful meal!

This dish is a great low-carb alternative to traditional pasta and pairs wonderfully with the fresh tomato basil sauce.

Turkey and Spinach Meatballs

Ingredients:

- 1 lb (450 g) ground turkey
- 2 cups fresh spinach, finely chopped
- 1/2 cup breadcrumbs (whole wheat or gluten-free if preferred)
- 1/4 cup grated Parmesan cheese (optional, or a dairy-free alternative)
- 1/4 cup finely chopped onion
- 2 cloves garlic, minced
- 1 large egg
- 1 tablespoon olive oil
- 1 teaspoon dried oregano
- 1/2 teaspoon dried basil
- 1/4 teaspoon red pepper flakes (optional, for a bit of heat)
- Salt and pepper to taste

Instructions:

1. **Preheat Oven:**
   - Preheat your oven to 400°F (200°C). Line a baking sheet with parchment paper or lightly grease it.
2. **Prepare the Mixture:**
   - In a large bowl, combine the ground turkey, chopped spinach, breadcrumbs, Parmesan cheese (if using), chopped onion, minced garlic, egg, olive oil, oregano, basil, red pepper flakes (if using), salt, and pepper.
   - Mix until all ingredients are well combined. Avoid overmixing to keep the meatballs tender.
3. **Form the Meatballs:**
   - Use your hands or a cookie scoop to form the mixture into 1 to 1.5-inch meatballs. Place them on the prepared baking sheet.
4. **Bake:**
   - Bake in the preheated oven for 15-20 minutes, or until the meatballs are cooked through and have an internal temperature of 165°F (74°C). They should be browned on the outside and firm to the touch.
5. **Serve:**
   - Allow the meatballs to cool slightly before serving. They can be enjoyed on their own, with marinara sauce, or added to a salad or pasta dish.

Optional Serving Suggestions:

- Serve with marinara sauce and a sprinkle of extra Parmesan cheese.
- Add to a whole-grain pasta dish or alongside roasted vegetables for a complete meal.

- Enjoy as a protein-packed snack with a side of dipping sauce.

Enjoy your flavorful and healthy Turkey and Spinach Meatballs!

Lentil and Vegetable Soup

Ingredients:

- 1 tablespoon olive oil
- 1 medium onion, diced
- 2 cloves garlic, minced
- 2 medium carrots, diced
- 2 celery stalks, diced
- 1 red bell pepper, diced
- 1 cup dried green or brown lentils, rinsed and drained
- 1 can (14.5 oz) diced tomatoes (with juice)
- 6 cups vegetable broth (or water)
- 1 cup green beans, chopped
- 1 cup zucchini, diced
- 1 teaspoon ground cumin
- 1/2 teaspoon paprika
- 1/2 teaspoon dried thyme
- 1/2 teaspoon dried basil
- 1 bay leaf
- Salt and pepper to taste
- 2 cups fresh spinach or kale, chopped
- Juice of 1 lemon (optional, for brightness)

Instructions:

1. **Sauté the Vegetables:**
   - Heat olive oil in a large pot over medium heat. Add the diced onion and cook until softened, about 5 minutes.
   - Add the minced garlic and cook for an additional 30 seconds, until fragrant.
   - Stir in the carrots, celery, and red bell pepper. Cook for 5-7 minutes, until the vegetables begin to soften.
2. **Add Lentils and Liquid:**
   - Add the rinsed lentils to the pot and stir to combine.
   - Pour in the diced tomatoes with their juice and the vegetable broth. Stir well.
3. **Season and Simmer:**
   - Add the ground cumin, paprika, dried thyme, dried basil, bay leaf, salt, and pepper. Stir to incorporate.
   - Bring the soup to a boil, then reduce the heat to low. Cover and simmer for 25-30 minutes, or until the lentils are tender.
4. **Add Remaining Vegetables:**
   - Stir in the green beans and zucchini. Continue to simmer for an additional 10 minutes, until the green beans and zucchini are tender.

5. **Finish the Soup:**
    - Remove the bay leaf from the pot.
    - Stir in the chopped spinach or kale and cook for an additional 2-3 minutes, until wilted.
    - If desired, add the lemon juice to the soup to brighten the flavors.
6. **Serve:**
    - Taste and adjust seasoning with more salt and pepper if needed. Serve hot, and enjoy!

Optional Additions:

- Serve with a slice of crusty whole-grain bread.
- Top with a dollop of Greek yogurt or a sprinkle of grated Parmesan cheese.

This Lentil and Vegetable Soup is packed with flavor and nutrients, making it a perfect meal for any time of the year. Enjoy!

Cauliflower Fried Rice

Ingredients:

- 1 medium head of cauliflower (or about 4 cups cauliflower rice)
- 2 tablespoons sesame oil (or olive oil)
- 1 small onion, diced
- 2 cloves garlic, minced
- 1 cup mixed vegetables (such as peas, carrots, corn, or bell peppers)
- 2 large eggs, lightly beaten
- 3 green onions, sliced
- 2-3 tablespoons low-sodium soy sauce or tamari
- 1 tablespoon oyster sauce (optional, for added flavor)
- 1/2 teaspoon ground ginger (or 1 teaspoon fresh ginger, minced)
- 1/4 teaspoon red pepper flakes (optional, for heat)
- Salt and pepper to taste
- Fresh cilantro or additional green onions for garnish (optional)

Instructions:

1. **Prepare Cauliflower Rice:**
   - Remove the leaves and stem from the cauliflower. Cut it into florets.
   - Pulse the florets in a food processor until it resembles rice. Alternatively, you can grate the cauliflower using a box grater. Set aside.
2. **Cook the Vegetables:**
   - Heat sesame oil in a large skillet or wok over medium-high heat.
   - Add the diced onion and cook for 3-4 minutes, until softened.
   - Add the minced garlic and cook for another 30 seconds until fragrant.
3. **Add Mixed Vegetables:**
   - Stir in the mixed vegetables and cook for 3-5 minutes, until they start to soften.
4. **Scramble the Eggs:**
   - Push the vegetables to one side of the skillet. Pour the beaten eggs into the empty side and scramble until cooked through. Once cooked, mix with the vegetables.
5. **Add Cauliflower Rice:**
   - Add the cauliflower rice to the skillet. Stir well to combine with the vegetables and eggs.
6. **Season:**
   - Pour the soy sauce (and oyster sauce, if using) over the cauliflower rice. Add ground ginger and red pepper flakes (if using). Stir well to ensure everything is evenly coated and heated through.
   - Cook for 5-7 minutes, stirring frequently, until the cauliflower rice is tender but not mushy.

7. **Finish and Serve:**
    - Stir in the sliced green onions. Taste and adjust seasoning with salt and pepper if needed.
    - Garnish with fresh cilantro or additional green onions if desired.

Optional Additions:

- Add cooked chicken, shrimp, or tofu for extra protein.
- Toss in some chopped cashews or sesame seeds for added texture.

This Cauliflower Fried Rice is a low-carb, veggie-packed alternative to traditional fried rice and makes for a great side dish or a complete meal on its own. Enjoy!

Greek Chicken Salad

Ingredients:

For the Salad:

- 2 cups cooked chicken breast, diced or shredded (can be grilled, baked, or rotisserie)
- 1 large cucumber, diced
- 1 cup cherry tomatoes, halved
- 1/2 red onion, thinly sliced
- 1/2 cup Kalamata olives, pitted and halved
- 1/2 cup feta cheese, crumbled (or a dairy-free alternative)
- 1/4 cup fresh parsley or basil, chopped

For the Dressing:

- 1/4 cup extra-virgin olive oil
- 2 tablespoons red wine vinegar
- 1 tablespoon lemon juice
- 1 clove garlic, minced
- 1 teaspoon dried oregano
- 1/2 teaspoon dried basil (optional)
- Salt and pepper to taste

Instructions:

1. **Prepare the Dressing:**
    - In a small bowl or jar, whisk together the olive oil, red wine vinegar, lemon juice, minced garlic, dried oregano, and dried basil (if using). Season with salt and pepper to taste. Set aside.
2. **Assemble the Salad:**
    - In a large bowl, combine the cooked chicken, diced cucumber, cherry tomatoes, sliced red onion, Kalamata olives, and crumbled feta cheese.
3. **Add the Dressing:**
    - Pour the prepared dressing over the salad ingredients. Toss gently to combine and coat everything evenly.
4. **Garnish and Serve:**
    - Sprinkle chopped parsley or basil on top for added freshness.
    - Serve immediately or refrigerate for 30 minutes to let the flavors meld.

Optional Additions:

- Add some sliced avocado or roasted red peppers for extra flavor.
- Serve the salad over a bed of mixed greens or alongside pita bread.

This Greek Chicken Salad is perfect for a light lunch or dinner and offers a delicious mix of flavors and textures. Enjoy!

Baked Cod with Lemon and Herbs

Ingredients:

- 4 cod fillets (6 oz each)
- 2 tablespoons olive oil
- 1 lemon, sliced
- 3 cloves garlic, minced
- 1 teaspoon dried thyme (or 1 tablespoon fresh thyme leaves)
- 1 teaspoon dried oregano (or 1 tablespoon fresh oregano leaves)
- 1/2 teaspoon paprika
- Salt and pepper to taste
- Fresh parsley or additional lemon slices for garnish (optional)

Instructions:

1. **Preheat Oven:**
   - Preheat your oven to 400°F (200°C). Line a baking sheet with parchment paper or lightly grease it.
2. **Prepare the Cod:**
   - Pat the cod fillets dry with paper towels. This helps the seasonings stick and ensures the fish bakes evenly.
   - Place the cod fillets on the prepared baking sheet.
3. **Season the Cod:**
   - Drizzle olive oil over the fillets.
   - Sprinkle minced garlic, dried thyme, dried oregano, paprika, salt, and pepper evenly over the fish.
   - Place lemon slices on top of or around the fillets.
4. **Bake:**
   - Bake in the preheated oven for 12-15 minutes, or until the cod is opaque and flakes easily with a fork. The cooking time may vary depending on the thickness of the fillets.
5. **Serve:**
   - Remove the cod from the oven and let it rest for a couple of minutes.
   - Garnish with fresh parsley or additional lemon slices if desired.

Optional Sides:

- Serve with steamed vegetables, a fresh green salad, or a side of quinoa or brown rice for a complete meal.

This Baked Cod with Lemon and Herbs is a light, healthy dish that's full of flavor and very easy to prepare. Enjoy!

Chickpea and Spinach Curry

Ingredients:

- 1 tablespoon olive oil or coconut oil
- 1 medium onion, finely chopped
- 2 cloves garlic, minced
- 1 tablespoon fresh ginger, minced
- 1 large tomato, diced (or 1 can (14.5 oz) diced tomatoes)
- 1 can (15 oz) chickpeas, drained and rinsed
- 2 cups fresh spinach leaves (or 1 cup frozen spinach, thawed and drained)
- 1 can (14 oz) coconut milk
- 1 tablespoon curry powder
- 1 teaspoon ground cumin
- 1/2 teaspoon ground turmeric
- 1/2 teaspoon paprika
- 1/4 teaspoon cayenne pepper (optional, for heat)
- Salt and pepper to taste
- 1 tablespoon lemon juice (optional, for brightness)
- Fresh cilantro for garnish (optional)

Instructions:

1. **Sauté Aromatics:**
    - Heat oil in a large skillet or saucepan over medium heat. Add the chopped onion and cook until softened and translucent, about 5 minutes.
    - Add minced garlic and ginger. Cook for an additional 1 minute until fragrant.
2. **Add Tomatoes and Spices:**
    - Stir in the diced tomatoes and cook for about 5 minutes until they begin to break down.
    - Add the curry powder, ground cumin, turmeric, paprika, and cayenne pepper (if using). Stir well to coat the onions and tomatoes with the spices.
3. **Incorporate Chickpeas and Spinach:**
    - Add the chickpeas to the skillet and stir to combine with the tomato and spice mixture.
    - Pour in the coconut milk and stir well.
    - Bring the mixture to a simmer and cook for about 10 minutes, allowing the flavors to meld and the sauce to thicken slightly.
4. **Add Spinach:**
    - Stir in the fresh spinach leaves and cook until wilted. If using frozen spinach, make sure it's well incorporated and heated through.
5. **Season and Finish:**

- Season with salt and pepper to taste. If desired, add a tablespoon of lemon juice to brighten the flavors.
6. **Serve:**
    - Garnish with fresh cilantro if desired.
    - Serve the curry hot over basmati rice, quinoa, or with naan bread.

Optional Additions:

- Add diced bell peppers or peas for extra veggies.
- Top with a dollop of Greek yogurt or a sprinkle of chopped nuts for added texture.

This Chickpea and Spinach Curry is rich, creamy, and packed with nutrients, making it a perfect choice for a wholesome meal. Enjoy!

Shrimp and Broccoli Skewers

Ingredients:

- 1 lb (450 g) large shrimp, peeled and deveined
- 2 cups broccoli florets
- 2 tablespoons olive oil
- 2 cloves garlic, minced
- 1 tablespoon lemon juice
- 1 teaspoon paprika
- 1 teaspoon dried oregano
- 1/2 teaspoon ground cumin
- Salt and pepper to taste
- Lemon wedges for serving (optional)
- Fresh parsley for garnish (optional)

Instructions:

1. **Prepare the Marinade:**
   - In a large bowl, combine olive oil, minced garlic, lemon juice, paprika, dried oregano, ground cumin, salt, and pepper. Mix well.
2. **Marinate the Shrimp:**
   - Add the shrimp to the bowl and toss to coat evenly with the marinade. Let it marinate for at least 15 minutes, or up to 1 hour in the refrigerator for more flavor.
3. **Prepare the Broccoli:**
   - While the shrimp is marinating, blanch the broccoli florets in boiling water for 2-3 minutes until they are bright green and slightly tender. Immediately transfer them to a bowl of ice water to stop the cooking process. Drain and pat dry.
4. **Assemble the Skewers:**
   - Thread the marinated shrimp and blanched broccoli onto skewers, alternating between shrimp and broccoli. If using wooden skewers, make sure to soak them in water for at least 30 minutes before using to prevent burning.
5. **Grill the Skewers:**
   - Preheat your grill or grill pan to medium-high heat.
   - Place the skewers on the grill and cook for about 2-3 minutes per side, or until the shrimp are opaque and cooked through and the broccoli is slightly charred. Be careful not to overcook the shrimp.
6. **Serve:**
   - Remove the skewers from the grill and let them rest for a couple of minutes.
   - Garnish with fresh parsley and serve with lemon wedges if desired.

Optional Side Suggestions:

- Serve with a side of quinoa, rice, or a fresh salad.
- Pair with a yogurt-based dipping sauce or tzatziki for extra flavor.

These Shrimp and Broccoli Skewers are perfect for a healthy and flavorful meal, ideal for grilling season or a quick weeknight dinner. Enjoy!

Stuffed Acorn Squash

Ingredients:

- 2 acorn squashes
- 1 tablespoon olive oil
- 1/2 cup quinoa or brown rice (uncooked)
- 1 cup vegetable broth or water (for cooking quinoa or rice)
- 1/2 cup diced onion
- 2 cloves garlic, minced
- 1 cup mushrooms, chopped
- 1 cup spinach, chopped (or kale)
- 1/2 cup dried cranberries or raisins
- 1/4 cup chopped nuts (such as walnuts or pecans)
- 1/4 cup crumbled feta cheese or a dairy-free alternative
- 1 teaspoon dried thyme
- 1/2 teaspoon dried sage
- Salt and pepper to taste
- Fresh parsley for garnish (optional)

Instructions:

1. **Preheat Oven:**
   - Preheat your oven to 400°F (200°C).
2. **Prepare the Acorn Squash:**
   - Cut the acorn squashes in half lengthwise and scoop out the seeds.
   - Brush the cut sides with olive oil and season with salt and pepper.
   - Place the squash halves cut-side down on a baking sheet lined with parchment paper or foil.
   - Roast in the preheated oven for 25-30 minutes, or until the flesh is tender when pierced with a fork.
3. **Cook the Quinoa or Rice:**
   - While the squash is roasting, cook the quinoa or brown rice according to package instructions, using vegetable broth or water.
4. **Prepare the Stuffing:**
   - Heat olive oil in a large skillet over medium heat.
   - Add diced onion and cook until softened, about 5 minutes.
   - Stir in the minced garlic and cook for an additional 30 seconds until fragrant.
   - Add the chopped mushrooms and cook until tender, about 5 minutes.
   - Stir in the chopped spinach and cook until wilted.
   - Mix in the dried cranberries or raisins, chopped nuts, cooked quinoa or rice, crumbled feta cheese, dried thyme, and dried sage. Season with salt and pepper to taste.

5. **Stuff the Squash:**
   - Remove the roasted squash from the oven and carefully turn them cut-side up.
   - Spoon the prepared stuffing into each squash half, packing it gently.
6. **Finish Baking:**
   - Return the stuffed squash to the oven and bake for an additional 10-15 minutes, or until the stuffing is heated through and the tops are slightly golden.
7. **Serve:**
   - Garnish with fresh parsley if desired.
   - Serve warm as a hearty main dish or a flavorful side.

Optional Additions:

- Add cooked ground turkey or sausage to the stuffing mixture for extra protein.
- Top with additional cheese before the final bake for a cheesy crust.

This Stuffed Acorn Squash recipe is perfect for a cozy fall meal or a festive holiday dish, combining savory and sweet flavors in a beautiful presentation. Enjoy!

Teriyaki Chicken and Veggie Bowl

Ingredients:

For the Chicken:

- 1 lb (450 g) boneless, skinless chicken thighs or breasts, cut into bite-sized pieces
- 2 tablespoons olive oil or sesame oil

For the Teriyaki Sauce:

- 1/4 cup low-sodium soy sauce or tamari
- 2 tablespoons honey or maple syrup
- 2 tablespoons rice vinegar
- 1 tablespoon grated fresh ginger (or 1 teaspoon ground ginger)
- 2 cloves garlic, minced
- 1 tablespoon cornstarch mixed with 1 tablespoon water (optional, for thickening)

For the Veggies:

- 1 cup broccoli florets
- 1 red bell pepper, sliced
- 1 cup snap peas
- 1 medium carrot, sliced thinly

For Serving:

- 2 cups cooked brown rice, quinoa, or cauliflower rice
- Sesame seeds (optional, for garnish)
- Sliced green onions (optional, for garnish)
- Fresh cilantro (optional, for garnish)

Instructions:

1. **Prepare the Teriyaki Sauce:**
   - In a small saucepan, combine soy sauce, honey (or maple syrup), rice vinegar, grated ginger, and minced garlic. Bring to a simmer over medium heat.
   - If you prefer a thicker sauce, stir in the cornstarch mixture and cook for an additional 1-2 minutes until the sauce has thickened. Remove from heat and set aside.
2. **Cook the Chicken:**
   - Heat olive oil or sesame oil in a large skillet or wok over medium-high heat.
   - Add the chicken pieces and cook until browned and cooked through, about 6-8 minutes. Stir occasionally to ensure even cooking.

3. **Add the Sauce:**
    - Pour the prepared teriyaki sauce over the cooked chicken. Stir to coat the chicken evenly and let it simmer for 1-2 minutes, allowing the sauce to meld with the chicken. Remove from heat.
4. **Cook the Veggies:**
    - In a separate skillet or pan, heat a small amount of oil over medium heat.
    - Add the broccoli, bell pepper, snap peas, and carrot. Stir-fry for 4-5 minutes, or until the vegetables are tender-crisp.
5. **Assemble the Bowl:**
    - Divide the cooked brown rice, quinoa, or cauliflower rice among serving bowls.
    - Top each bowl with a portion of the teriyaki chicken and a generous serving of the stir-fried vegetables.
6. **Garnish and Serve:**
    - Garnish with sesame seeds, sliced green onions, and fresh cilantro if desired.
    - Serve warm and enjoy!

Optional Additions:

- Add a side of pickled ginger or a drizzle of sriracha for extra flavor.
- Include some avocado slices for added creaminess.

This Teriyaki Chicken and Veggie Bowl is a complete and satisfying meal that's full of flavor and packed with nutritious ingredients. Enjoy!

Spicy Black Bean Tacos

Ingredients:

For the Black Beans:

- 2 cans (15 oz each) black beans, drained and rinsed
- 1 tablespoon olive oil
- 1 medium onion, finely chopped
- 2 cloves garlic, minced
- 1 bell pepper (red or green), diced
- 1 teaspoon ground cumin
- 1 teaspoon smoked paprika
- 1/2 teaspoon chili powder
- 1/4 teaspoon cayenne pepper (optional, for extra heat)
- Salt and pepper to taste
- 1/2 cup water or vegetable broth

For Serving:

- 8 small corn or flour tortillas
- 1 cup shredded lettuce
- 1 cup diced tomatoes
- 1 avocado, sliced or diced
- 1/2 cup crumbled feta cheese or a dairy-free alternative
- Fresh cilantro, chopped (for garnish)
- Lime wedges (for serving)
- Salsa or hot sauce (optional)

Instructions:

1. **Prepare the Black Beans:**
    - Heat olive oil in a large skillet over medium heat.
    - Add the chopped onion and cook until softened, about 5 minutes.
    - Stir in the minced garlic and cook for an additional 30 seconds until fragrant.
    - Add the diced bell pepper and cook for another 3-4 minutes until tender.
2. **Season the Beans:**
    - Stir in the drained black beans, ground cumin, smoked paprika, chili powder, and cayenne pepper (if using). Mix well.
    - Pour in the water or vegetable broth and stir to combine.
    - Let the mixture simmer for 5-7 minutes, until heated through and slightly thickened. Season with salt and pepper to taste.
3. **Prepare the Tortillas:**

- While the beans are simmering, warm the tortillas. You can do this in a dry skillet over medium heat for about 30 seconds per side, or wrap them in foil and warm them in the oven.

4. **Assemble the Tacos:**
   - Spoon the spicy black bean mixture onto each tortilla.
   - Top with shredded lettuce, diced tomatoes, avocado slices, and crumbled feta cheese.
5. **Garnish and Serve:**
   - Garnish with fresh cilantro and a squeeze of lime juice.
   - Serve with salsa or hot sauce on the side if desired.

Optional Additions:

- Add a dollop of Greek yogurt or sour cream for creaminess.
- Include sliced jalapeños or pickled onions for extra zing.

These Spicy Black Bean Tacos are a flavorful and nutritious option, perfect for a quick weeknight dinner or a fun weekend meal. Enjoy!

Grilled Portobello Mushrooms with Quinoa

Ingredients:

For the Portobello Mushrooms:

- 4 large Portobello mushrooms, stems removed
- 2 tablespoons olive oil
- 2 cloves garlic, minced
- 1 tablespoon balsamic vinegar
- 1 teaspoon dried oregano
- 1/2 teaspoon dried thyme
- Salt and pepper to taste

For the Quinoa:

- 1 cup quinoa
- 2 cups vegetable broth or water
- 1 tablespoon olive oil
- 1 small onion, finely chopped
- 1 red bell pepper, diced
- 1 cup cherry tomatoes, halved
- 1 cup fresh spinach or kale, chopped
- 1/4 cup fresh basil or parsley, chopped
- Salt and pepper to taste

Instructions:

1. **Prepare the Quinoa:**
   - Rinse the quinoa under cold water in a fine mesh strainer.
   - In a medium saucepan, bring vegetable broth or water to a boil.
   - Add quinoa, reduce heat to low, cover, and simmer for 15 minutes, or until the quinoa is tender and the liquid is absorbed. Remove from heat and let it sit, covered, for 5 minutes.
   - Fluff with a fork and set aside.
2. **Prepare the Portobello Mushrooms:**
   - In a small bowl, whisk together olive oil, minced garlic, balsamic vinegar, dried oregano, dried thyme, salt, and pepper.
   - Brush the mushroom caps with the marinade on both sides.
3. **Grill the Mushrooms:**
   - Preheat your grill to medium-high heat.
   - Place the mushrooms on the grill, gill side down, and cook for about 4-5 minutes per side, or until they are tender and have grill marks. Brush with additional marinade if desired.

4. **Prepare the Quinoa Mix:**
    - While the mushrooms are grilling, heat 1 tablespoon olive oil in a large skillet over medium heat.
    - Add the chopped onion and cook until softened, about 5 minutes.
    - Stir in the diced red bell pepper and cook for an additional 3-4 minutes.
    - Add the cherry tomatoes and cook for 2 minutes, until they start to soften.
    - Stir in the chopped spinach or kale and cook until wilted.
    - Mix in the cooked quinoa and chopped fresh basil or parsley. Season with salt and pepper to taste.
5. **Assemble and Serve:**
    - Slice the grilled Portobello mushrooms and place them on serving plates.
    - Spoon the quinoa mixture alongside or underneath the mushrooms.
    - Garnish with additional fresh herbs if desired.

Optional Additions:

- Add crumbled feta cheese or a sprinkle of nutritional yeast for extra flavor.
- Serve with a side salad or roasted vegetables for a complete meal.

These Grilled Portobello Mushrooms with Quinoa make for a satisfying and flavorful meal that's perfect for a light lunch or dinner. Enjoy!

Mediterranean Quinoa Salad

Ingredients:

- 1 cup quinoa, rinsed
- 2 cups water or vegetable broth
- 1 cup cherry tomatoes, halved
- 1 cucumber, diced
- 1/2 red onion, finely chopped
- 1/2 cup Kalamata olives, pitted and sliced
- 1/2 cup crumbled feta cheese (or a dairy-free alternative)
- 1/4 cup fresh parsley, chopped
- 1/4 cup fresh mint, chopped (optional)

For the Dressing:

- 1/4 cup extra-virgin olive oil
- 3 tablespoons red wine vinegar
- 1 tablespoon lemon juice
- 1 clove garlic, minced
- 1 teaspoon dried oregano
- 1/2 teaspoon dried basil
- Salt and pepper to taste

Instructions:

1. **Cook the Quinoa:**
   - In a medium saucepan, bring water or vegetable broth to a boil.
   - Add the rinsed quinoa, reduce heat to low, cover, and simmer for about 15 minutes, or until the quinoa is tender and the liquid is absorbed.
   - Remove from heat and let it sit, covered, for 5 minutes. Fluff with a fork and let it cool to room temperature.
2. **Prepare the Vegetables:**
   - While the quinoa is cooking, chop the cherry tomatoes, cucumber, red onion, and olives.
3. **Make the Dressing:**
   - In a small bowl, whisk together olive oil, red wine vinegar, lemon juice, minced garlic, dried oregano, dried basil, salt, and pepper.
4. **Assemble the Salad:**
   - In a large bowl, combine the cooked quinoa, cherry tomatoes, cucumber, red onion, Kalamata olives, crumbled feta cheese, and chopped parsley (and mint if using).
5. **Add the Dressing:**

- Pour the dressing over the salad and toss gently to coat all ingredients evenly.
6. **Serve:**
    - Serve the salad immediately or refrigerate for about 30 minutes to allow the flavors to meld.

Optional Additions:

- Add grilled chicken or chickpeas for extra protein.
- Top with avocado slices or a sprinkle of pine nuts for added richness.

This Mediterranean Quinoa Salad is light, nutritious, and packed with fresh flavors, making it a great option for a healthy lunch or a side dish at dinner. Enjoy!

Baked Chicken Parmesan

Ingredients:

- 4 boneless, skinless chicken breasts
- 1 cup whole wheat breadcrumbs or panko breadcrumbs
- 1/2 cup grated Parmesan cheese
- 1 teaspoon dried Italian seasoning
- 1/2 teaspoon garlic powder
- 1/2 teaspoon onion powder
- 1/2 teaspoon paprika
- Salt and pepper to taste
- 1/2 cup all-purpose flour
- 2 large eggs, beaten
- 1 cup marinara sauce (low-sodium if preferred)
- 1 cup shredded mozzarella cheese (or a dairy-free alternative)
- Fresh basil or parsley for garnish (optional)

Instructions:

1. **Preheat Oven:**
   - Preheat your oven to 400°F (200°C). Line a baking sheet with parchment paper or lightly grease it.
2. **Prepare the Breading:**
   - In a shallow dish, mix the breadcrumbs, grated Parmesan cheese, dried Italian seasoning, garlic powder, onion powder, paprika, salt, and pepper.
3. **Bread the Chicken:**
   - Dredge each chicken breast in flour, shaking off any excess.
   - Dip the floured chicken into the beaten eggs, allowing any excess to drip off.
   - Coat the chicken with the breadcrumb mixture, pressing lightly to ensure the coating sticks.
4. **Bake the Chicken:**
   - Place the breaded chicken breasts on the prepared baking sheet.
   - Bake in the preheated oven for 20-25 minutes, or until the chicken is cooked through and the internal temperature reaches 165°F (74°C). The chicken should be golden brown and crispy.
5. **Add Marinara Sauce and Cheese:**
   - Remove the chicken from the oven and spoon a few tablespoons of marinara sauce over each breast.
   - Sprinkle shredded mozzarella cheese on top of the sauce.
6. **Finish Baking:**
   - Return the chicken to the oven and bake for an additional 5-7 minutes, or until the cheese is melted and bubbly.

7. **Garnish and Serve:**
    - Garnish with fresh basil or parsley if desired.
    - Serve the Baked Chicken Parmesan with a side of whole grain pasta, a fresh salad, or steamed vegetables.

Optional Additions:

- For extra flavor, sprinkle some red pepper flakes over the chicken before baking.
- Add a side of roasted garlic or sautéed spinach for a complete meal.

This Baked Chicken Parmesan is a healthier alternative to the traditional fried version, maintaining all the delicious flavors with less fat and fewer calories. Enjoy!

Roasted Vegetable and Hummus Wrap

Ingredients:

For the Roasted Vegetables:

- 1 red bell pepper, sliced
- 1 zucchini, sliced
- 1 small red onion, sliced
- 1 cup cherry tomatoes, halved
- 2 tablespoons olive oil
- 1 teaspoon dried oregano
- 1 teaspoon dried thyme
- Salt and pepper to taste

For the Wrap:

- 4 large whole wheat or spinach tortillas
- 1 cup hummus (store-bought or homemade)
- 1 cup fresh spinach or mixed greens
- 1/4 cup crumbled feta cheese or a dairy-free alternative (optional)
- 1/4 cup sliced black olives (optional)
- Fresh lemon juice (optional, for added brightness)

Instructions:

1. **Roast the Vegetables:**
    - Preheat your oven to 400°F (200°C).
    - On a large baking sheet, toss the red bell pepper, zucchini, red onion, and cherry tomatoes with olive oil, dried oregano, dried thyme, salt, and pepper.
    - Spread the vegetables in an even layer on the baking sheet.
    - Roast in the preheated oven for 20-25 minutes, or until the vegetables are tender and slightly caramelized. Stir halfway through for even roasting.
2. **Prepare the Wraps:**
    - While the vegetables are roasting, prepare the wraps. If desired, warm the tortillas slightly in a dry skillet over medium heat or in the oven to make them more pliable.
3. **Assemble the Wraps:**
    - Spread a generous layer of hummus over each tortilla.
    - Top with a portion of the roasted vegetables.
    - Add fresh spinach or mixed greens on top of the vegetables.
    - Sprinkle with crumbled feta cheese and sliced black olives if using.
    - Drizzle with a little fresh lemon juice for added flavor, if desired.
4. **Wrap and Serve:**

    - Roll up each tortilla tightly, folding in the sides as you go to enclose the filling.
    - Cut the wraps in half if desired for easier handling.

Optional Additions:

- Add sliced avocado for extra creaminess.
- Include cooked quinoa or chickpeas for added protein and texture.

These Roasted Vegetable and Hummus Wraps are perfect for a quick and healthy lunch or dinner, packed with flavor and nutrients. Enjoy!

Miso Glazed Eggplant

Ingredients:

- 2 medium eggplants
- 2 tablespoons olive oil
- 2 tablespoons white miso paste (or red miso for a stronger flavor)
- 2 tablespoons soy sauce or tamari
- 2 tablespoons maple syrup or honey
- 1 tablespoon rice vinegar
- 1 tablespoon sesame oil
- 2 cloves garlic, minced
- 1 teaspoon freshly grated ginger
- 1 teaspoon sesame seeds (optional, for garnish)
- 2 green onions, sliced (optional, for garnish)
- Fresh cilantro (optional, for garnish)

Instructions:

1. **Prepare the Eggplant:**
   - Preheat your oven to 425°F (220°C).
   - Cut the eggplants in half lengthwise and score the flesh in a crisscross pattern, being careful not to cut through the skin.
2. **Make the Miso Glaze:**
   - In a small bowl, whisk together the miso paste, soy sauce or tamari, maple syrup or honey, rice vinegar, sesame oil, minced garlic, and grated ginger until smooth.
3. **Glaze the Eggplant:**
   - Brush the cut sides of the eggplant with olive oil and place them cut-side up on a baking sheet.
   - Spread the miso glaze evenly over the cut sides of the eggplants.
4. **Roast the Eggplant:**
   - Roast in the preheated oven for 25-30 minutes, or until the eggplant is tender and the glaze is caramelized. The edges should be golden brown and slightly crispy.
5. **Garnish and Serve:**
   - Remove from the oven and let cool slightly.
   - Sprinkle with sesame seeds, sliced green onions, and fresh cilantro if desired.

Optional Additions:

- Serve with a side of steamed rice or quinoa for a complete meal.
- Add a drizzle of additional sesame oil or a splash of extra soy sauce for extra flavor.

This Miso Glazed Eggplant is a savory and slightly sweet dish that pairs well with a variety of sides and makes for a delicious and nutritious addition to any meal. Enjoy!

Turkey and Sweet Potato Chili

Ingredients:

- 1 tablespoon olive oil
- 1 lb (450 g) ground turkey
- 1 medium onion, chopped
- 2 cloves garlic, minced
- 1 red bell pepper, chopped
- 1 green bell pepper, chopped
- 1 large sweet potato, peeled and diced
- 1 can (14.5 oz) diced tomatoes
- 1 can (15 oz) kidney beans, drained and rinsed
- 1 can (15 oz) black beans, drained and rinsed
- 1 cup low-sodium chicken broth
- 2 tablespoons chili powder
- 1 teaspoon ground cumin
- 1/2 teaspoon smoked paprika
- 1/4 teaspoon cayenne pepper (optional, for heat)
- Salt and pepper to taste
- 1 cup frozen corn (optional)
- Fresh cilantro or parsley for garnish (optional)
- Lime wedges for serving (optional)

Instructions:

1. **Cook the Turkey:**
   - Heat olive oil in a large pot or Dutch oven over medium heat.
   - Add ground turkey and cook until browned, breaking it up with a spoon as it cooks. Drain any excess fat if necessary.
2. **Sauté Vegetables:**
   - Add chopped onion and cook until softened, about 5 minutes.
   - Stir in minced garlic and cook for an additional 30 seconds until fragrant.
3. **Add Sweet Potato and Peppers:**
   - Add diced sweet potato, red bell pepper, and green bell pepper to the pot. Cook for 5-7 minutes, stirring occasionally, until the vegetables start to soften.
4. **Add Remaining Ingredients:**
   - Stir in the diced tomatoes, kidney beans, black beans, and chicken broth.
   - Add chili powder, ground cumin, smoked paprika, cayenne pepper (if using), salt, and pepper. Stir well to combine.
5. **Simmer the Chili:**
   - Bring the mixture to a boil, then reduce heat to low and let it simmer for 20-25 minutes, or until the sweet potatoes are tender and the chili has thickened. Stir occasionally.
   - If using frozen corn, add it during the last 5 minutes of cooking.

6. **Adjust Seasoning and Serve:**
    - Taste and adjust seasoning with additional salt, pepper, or chili powder if needed.
    - Garnish with fresh cilantro or parsley if desired.
    - Serve with lime wedges on the side for added brightness.

Optional Toppings:

- Shredded cheese
- Sliced jalapeños
- Greek yogurt or sour cream
- Avocado slices

This Turkey and Sweet Potato Chili is a nutritious, flavorful dish that's perfect for a cozy dinner. It's packed with protein, fiber, and a comforting blend of spices. Enjoy!

Spinach and Feta Stuffed Chicken Breast

Ingredients:

- 4 boneless, skinless chicken breasts
- 1 tablespoon olive oil
- 2 cups fresh spinach, chopped
- 1/2 cup crumbled feta cheese
- 1/4 cup sun-dried tomatoes, chopped (optional)
- 2 cloves garlic, minced
- 1/4 teaspoon dried oregano
- 1/4 teaspoon dried thyme
- Salt and pepper to taste
- Toothpicks or kitchen twine for securing

Instructions:

1. **Preheat Oven:**
   - Preheat your oven to 375°F (190°C).
2. **Prepare the Filling:**
   - In a medium skillet, heat olive oil over medium heat.
   - Add the minced garlic and cook for about 30 seconds until fragrant.
   - Add the chopped spinach and cook until wilted and the liquid has evaporated, about 2-3 minutes.
   - Remove from heat and stir in the crumbled feta cheese and sun-dried tomatoes if using. Season with dried oregano, dried thyme, salt, and pepper. Mix well and set aside.
3. **Prepare the Chicken:**
   - Place each chicken breast between two sheets of plastic wrap or parchment paper. Gently pound the chicken with a meat mallet or rolling pin until it is even in thickness, about 1/2 inch thick.
4. **Stuff the Chicken:**
   - Remove the plastic wrap or parchment paper. Place a generous amount of the spinach and feta mixture in the center of each chicken breast.
   - Fold the sides of the chicken over the filling, then roll it up tightly. Secure the rolled chicken with toothpicks or tie with kitchen twine to keep the filling inside.
5. **Cook the Chicken:**
   - Heat a large, oven-safe skillet over medium-high heat. Add a small amount of olive oil.
   - Sear the chicken rolls on all sides until golden brown, about 2-3 minutes per side.
   - Transfer the skillet to the preheated oven and bake for 20-25 minutes, or until the chicken is cooked through and the internal temperature reaches 165°F (74°C).
6. **Serve:**
   - Remove the chicken from the oven and let it rest for a few minutes before removing the toothpicks or twine.
   - Slice and serve with your choice of side dishes, such as roasted vegetables, quinoa, or a fresh salad.

Optional Additions:

- Top with a light tomato sauce or a sprinkle of additional feta cheese before serving.
- Add a squeeze of lemon juice over the chicken for extra brightness.

This Spinach and Feta Stuffed Chicken Breast is a flavorful, protein-packed meal that's perfect for a weeknight dinner or special occasion. Enjoy!

Butternut Squash Risotto

Ingredients:

- 1 medium butternut squash, peeled, seeded, and diced
- 2 tablespoons olive oil, divided
- 1 small onion, finely chopped
- 2 cloves garlic, minced
- 1 1/2 cups Arborio rice
- 1/2 cup dry white wine (optional)
- 4 cups low-sodium vegetable broth (or chicken broth), kept warm
- 1/2 cup grated Parmesan cheese (or a dairy-free alternative)
- 1/4 cup chopped fresh sage or thyme (or 1 teaspoon dried sage/thyme)
- Salt and pepper to taste
- 2 tablespoons butter (optional, for added creaminess)
- Fresh parsley or additional sage for garnish (optional)

Instructions:

1. **Roast the Butternut Squash:**
   - Preheat your oven to 400°F (200°C).
   - Toss the diced butternut squash with 1 tablespoon of olive oil, salt, and pepper.
   - Spread in a single layer on a baking sheet.
   - Roast for 25-30 minutes, or until tender and caramelized, stirring halfway through. Set aside.
2. **Prepare the Risotto:**
   - In a large skillet or saucepan, heat the remaining 1 tablespoon of olive oil over medium heat.
   - Add the chopped onion and cook until softened, about 5 minutes.
   - Stir in the minced garlic and cook for an additional 30 seconds until fragrant.
3. **Cook the Rice:**
   - Add the Arborio rice to the skillet and cook, stirring constantly, for 1-2 minutes until the rice is lightly toasted.
   - If using white wine, pour it in and cook until the wine is mostly absorbed.
4. **Add Broth Gradually:**
   - Begin adding the warm vegetable broth to the rice, one ladleful at a time. Stir frequently and allow each addition to be absorbed before adding more broth.
   - Continue this process until the rice is creamy and cooked to al dente, about 18-20 minutes.
5. **Incorporate the Squash:**
   - Gently fold the roasted butternut squash into the risotto.
   - Stir in the grated Parmesan cheese and chopped fresh sage (or thyme).
   - If desired, stir in 2 tablespoons of butter for extra creaminess.
6. **Season and Serve:**
   - Taste and adjust seasoning with salt and pepper as needed.
   - Garnish with fresh parsley or additional sage if desired.

Optional Additions:

- For added protein, stir in some cooked chicken, shrimp, or beans.
- Top with extra Parmesan cheese or a drizzle of balsamic glaze for extra flavor.

This Butternut Squash Risotto is a rich, creamy dish with the natural sweetness of roasted squash and a touch of savory sage. It's perfect for a comforting meal on a cool evening. Enjoy!

Thai Peanut Chicken Lettuce Wraps

Ingredients:

For the Chicken Filling:

- 1 lb (450 g) ground chicken
- 1 tablespoon olive oil
- 1 small onion, finely chopped
- 2 cloves garlic, minced
- 1 red bell pepper, finely diced
- 1 cup shredded carrots
- 1/2 cup water chestnuts, diced (optional, for extra crunch)
- 1/4 cup chopped fresh cilantro or basil (optional)

For the Thai Peanut Sauce:

- 1/4 cup peanut butter (creamy or crunchy)
- 2 tablespoons soy sauce or tamari
- 2 tablespoons rice vinegar
- 1 tablespoon honey or maple syrup
- 1 tablespoon lime juice
- 1 teaspoon grated ginger
- 1-2 teaspoons sriracha or chili garlic sauce (optional, for heat)
- Water, as needed to thin the sauce

For Serving:

- 1 head of butter lettuce or iceberg lettuce, leaves separated and washed
- 1/4 cup chopped peanuts (optional, for garnish)
- Extra cilantro or basil for garnish (optional)
- Lime wedges for serving (optional)

Instructions:

1. **Prepare the Chicken Filling:**
    - Heat olive oil in a large skillet over medium heat.
    - Add the ground chicken and cook until browned and cooked through, breaking it up with a spoon as it cooks. Drain any excess fat if necessary.
    - Add the chopped onion and cook until softened, about 5 minutes.
    - Stir in the minced garlic and cook for another 30 seconds.
    - Add the diced red bell pepper, shredded carrots, and water chestnuts (if using). Cook for 3-4 minutes until the vegetables are tender-crisp.
    - Stir in the chopped cilantro or basil if desired. Set aside.
2. **Make the Thai Peanut Sauce:**
    - In a medium bowl, whisk together peanut butter, soy sauce, rice vinegar, honey or maple syrup, lime juice, grated ginger, and sriracha or chili garlic sauce if using.

- Gradually add water, a tablespoon at a time, until the sauce reaches your desired consistency (smooth and pourable).
3. **Assemble the Wraps:**
    - Spoon a portion of the chicken filling into the center of each lettuce leaf.
    - Drizzle with Thai peanut sauce.
4. **Garnish and Serve:**
    - Garnish with chopped peanuts and extra cilantro or basil if desired.
    - Serve with lime wedges on the side for added brightness.

Optional Additions:

- Add shredded cabbage or bean sprouts to the filling for extra crunch.
- Serve with extra Thai peanut sauce on the side for dipping.

These Thai Peanut Chicken Lettuce Wraps are perfect for a fresh, healthy, and flavorful meal. Enjoy the crunch of the lettuce with the savory-sweet peanut sauce and tender chicken filling!

Roasted Salmon with Asparagus

Ingredients:

- **For the salmon:**
    - 4 salmon fillets (about 6 oz each)
    - 2 tablespoons olive oil
    - 2 cloves garlic, minced
    - 1 lemon, sliced
    - Salt and pepper to taste
    - Fresh dill or parsley for garnish (optional)
- **For the asparagus:**
    - 1 bunch asparagus, trimmed
    - 1 tablespoon olive oil
    - 1/2 teaspoon garlic powder
    - Salt and pepper to taste
    - 1/2 teaspoon lemon zest (optional)

Instructions:

1. **Preheat the Oven:**
    - Preheat your oven to 400°F (200°C).
2. **Prepare the Salmon:**
    - Place the salmon fillets on a baking sheet lined with parchment paper or lightly greased.
    - Drizzle olive oil over the salmon fillets and rub it in evenly.
    - Sprinkle the minced garlic over the fillets.
    - Season with salt and pepper to taste.
    - Place lemon slices on top of each fillet.
    - If using, sprinkle fresh dill or parsley on top.
3. **Prepare the Asparagus:**
    - In a bowl, toss the asparagus with olive oil, garlic powder, salt, and pepper.
    - Arrange the asparagus on the same baking sheet as the salmon, or on a separate one if there's not enough space. If they are on the same sheet, try to keep them to the side of the salmon to ensure they roast properly.
4. **Roast:**
    - Place the baking sheet(s) in the oven.
    - Roast for about 15-20 minutes, or until the salmon flakes easily with a fork and the asparagus is tender and slightly crispy. The exact time will depend on the thickness of your salmon fillets and the size of the asparagus.
5. **Finish and Serve:**
    - Remove from the oven and let it rest for a few minutes.
    - Garnish with extra lemon slices or fresh herbs if desired.
    - Serve immediately.

This dish pairs wonderfully with a simple side salad or some quinoa for a complete meal. Enjoy your roasted salmon and asparagus!

Zucchini and Tomato Frittata

Ingredients:

- **For the frittata:**
    - 1 tablespoon olive oil

- 1 medium zucchini, sliced (or diced if you prefer)
- 1 cup cherry tomatoes, halved (or 1-2 regular tomatoes, diced)
- 1 small onion, diced
- 4 large eggs
- 1/4 cup milk or cream
- 1/2 cup shredded cheese (such as feta, cheddar, or goat cheese)
- Salt and pepper to taste
- 1/4 teaspoon dried oregano (optional)
- 1/4 teaspoon dried basil (optional)
- Fresh herbs for garnish (like parsley or basil, optional)

Instructions:

1. **Preheat the Oven:**
   - Preheat your oven to 375°F (190°C).
2. **Cook the Vegetables:**
   - Heat the olive oil in an oven-safe skillet (preferably cast iron) over medium heat.
   - Add the diced onion and cook until it becomes translucent, about 3-4 minutes.
   - Add the zucchini and cook for another 5 minutes until it starts to soften.
   - Stir in the cherry tomatoes and cook for an additional 2 minutes. Season with salt, pepper, and any dried herbs you're using.
3. **Prepare the Egg Mixture:**
   - In a bowl, whisk together the eggs and milk (or cream) until well combined.
   - Stir in the shredded cheese.
4. **Combine and Cook:**
   - Pour the egg mixture over the cooked vegetables in the skillet.
   - Stir gently to distribute the vegetables evenly.
   - Cook on the stovetop over medium heat for about 2-3 minutes, just until the edges start to set.
5. **Transfer to Oven:**
   - Transfer the skillet to the preheated oven.
   - Bake for 15-20 minutes, or until the frittata is fully set in the middle and lightly golden on top. A toothpick inserted into the center should come out clean.
6. **Finish and Serve:**
   - Let the frittata cool for a few minutes before slicing.
   - Garnish with fresh herbs if desired.
   - Serve warm or at room temperature.

This frittata is great on its own or with a side of mixed greens or a light salad. Enjoy!

Beef and Broccoli Stir-Fry

Ingredients:

- **For the Beef and Marinade:**
    - 1 lb (450g) flank steak or sirloin, thinly sliced against the grain
    - 2 tablespoons soy sauce
    - 1 tablespoon oyster sauce (optional)

- 1 tablespoon cornstarch
- 1 tablespoon vegetable oil (for marinating)
- **For the Stir-Fry:**
    - 2 tablespoons vegetable oil (for cooking)
    - 2-3 cups broccoli florets (about 1 medium head of broccoli)
    - 1 red bell pepper, sliced (optional)
    - 3 cloves garlic, minced
    - 1 tablespoon ginger, minced
    - 1/2 cup beef broth (or water)
    - 2 tablespoons soy sauce
    - 1 tablespoon oyster sauce (optional)
    - 1 tablespoon hoisin sauce (optional)
    - 1 teaspoon sesame oil (optional)
    - 1 tablespoon cornstarch mixed with 2 tablespoons water (for thickening sauce)

Instructions:

1. **Marinate the Beef:**
    - In a bowl, combine the sliced beef with 2 tablespoons soy sauce, 1 tablespoon oyster sauce (if using), 1 tablespoon cornstarch, and 1 tablespoon vegetable oil. Mix well and let it marinate for at least 15 minutes. For more flavor, marinate for up to an hour in the refrigerator.
2. **Prepare the Vegetables:**
    - While the beef is marinating, prepare your vegetables. Cut the broccoli into bite-sized florets and slice the red bell pepper if using.
3. **Stir-Fry the Beef:**
    - Heat 2 tablespoons vegetable oil in a large skillet or wok over high heat.
    - Add the marinated beef in a single layer. Let it sear without moving it for about 1-2 minutes until it's browned. Stir-fry the beef for another 2-3 minutes until it's cooked through. Remove the beef from the skillet and set it aside.
4. **Cook the Vegetables:**
    - In the same skillet, add a little more oil if needed. Add the broccoli florets and red bell pepper (if using). Stir-fry for about 3-4 minutes until the vegetables are tender-crisp.
    - Add the minced garlic and ginger. Stir-fry for an additional 30 seconds until fragrant.
5. **Combine and Sauce:**
    - Return the cooked beef to the skillet with the vegetables.
    - In a small bowl, mix together the beef broth, 2 tablespoons soy sauce, 1 tablespoon oyster sauce (if using), 1 tablespoon hoisin sauce (if using), and 1 teaspoon sesame oil (if using). Pour this sauce over the beef and vegetables.
    - Stir well to combine and bring the sauce to a simmer.
    - Add the cornstarch-water mixture to thicken the sauce. Stir constantly until the sauce has thickened to your liking, about 1-2 minutes.
6. **Finish and Serve:**

- Taste and adjust the seasoning with more soy sauce or pepper if needed.
- Serve the beef and broccoli stir-fry hot over steamed rice or noodles.

Enjoy your homemade beef and broccoli stir-fry! It's a great way to enjoy a flavorful, balanced meal.

Cauliflower and Chickpea Tacos

Ingredients:

- **For the Filling:**
    - 1 small head of cauliflower, cut into small florets
    - 1 can (15 oz) chickpeas, drained and rinsed
    - 2 tablespoons olive oil
    - 1 tablespoon chili powder
    - 1 teaspoon ground cumin

- 1/2 teaspoon smoked paprika
- 1/2 teaspoon garlic powder
- 1/2 teaspoon onion powder
- 1/4 teaspoon cayenne pepper (optional, for heat)
- Salt and pepper to taste
- **For the Tacos:**
  - 8 small tortillas (corn or flour)
  - 1 cup shredded lettuce or shredded cabbage
  - 1 cup diced tomatoes or salsa
  - 1/2 red onion, finely chopped
  - Fresh cilantro, chopped
  - Lime wedges
  - Avocado slices or guacamole (optional)
  - Sour cream or Greek yogurt (optional)

Instructions:

1. **Prepare the Filling:**
   - Preheat your oven to 425°F (220°C).
   - In a large bowl, toss the cauliflower florets and chickpeas with olive oil, chili powder, cumin, smoked paprika, garlic powder, onion powder, cayenne pepper (if using), salt, and pepper until everything is well coated.
   - Spread the mixture in a single layer on a baking sheet lined with parchment paper or lightly greased.
2. **Roast:**
   - Roast in the preheated oven for 25-30 minutes, stirring halfway through, until the cauliflower is tender and slightly crispy and the chickpeas are golden and crispy.
3. **Prepare the Toppings:**
   - While the filling is roasting, prepare your taco toppings. Shred the lettuce or cabbage, dice the tomatoes, chop the red onion and cilantro, and slice the avocado if using.
4. **Warm the Tortillas:**
   - Warm the tortillas in a dry skillet over medium heat for about 30 seconds per side, or wrap them in foil and warm them in the oven for a few minutes. Alternatively, you can microwave them between damp paper towels for about 20-30 seconds.
5. **Assemble the Tacos:**
   - Once the cauliflower and chickpeas are done, remove them from the oven.
   - Spoon the roasted cauliflower and chickpeas onto the warmed tortillas.
   - Top with shredded lettuce or cabbage, diced tomatoes or salsa, chopped red onion, and fresh cilantro.
   - Add avocado slices or a dollop of guacamole, and a spoonful of sour cream or Greek yogurt if desired.
   - Squeeze lime juice over the top to add a fresh, tangy flavor.
6. **Serve:**

- Serve the tacos immediately, while they're warm. Enjoy with extra lime wedges on the side for added zest.

These tacos are perfect for a quick weeknight dinner or a casual gathering. They're packed with flavor, fiber, and protein, making them both satisfying and nutritious.

Quinoa and Roasted Vegetable Bowl

Ingredients:

- **For the Quinoa:**
    - 1 cup quinoa
    - 2 cups water or vegetable broth
    - 1/2 teaspoon salt
- **For the Roasted Vegetables:**
    - 1 cup cherry tomatoes, halved
    - 1 bell pepper, diced
    - 1 zucchini, sliced

- 1 red onion, diced
- 2 tablespoons olive oil
- 1 teaspoon dried oregano
- 1 teaspoon dried basil
- Salt and pepper to taste
- **For the Dressing (Optional):**
    - 3 tablespoons olive oil
    - 2 tablespoons lemon juice
    - 1 tablespoon Dijon mustard
    - 1 teaspoon honey or maple syrup
    - Salt and pepper to taste
- **Toppings (Optional):**
    - Fresh herbs (like parsley or cilantro)
    - Feta cheese or crumbled goat cheese
    - Sliced avocado

Instructions:

1. **Cook the Quinoa:**
    - Rinse the quinoa under cold water.
    - In a medium saucepan, bring 2 cups of water or vegetable broth to a boil.
    - Add the quinoa and salt. Reduce the heat to low, cover, and simmer for about 15 minutes, or until the quinoa is cooked and the liquid is absorbed.
    - Fluff with a fork and set aside.
2. **Roast the Vegetables:**
    - Preheat your oven to 425°F (220°C).
    - On a baking sheet, toss the cherry tomatoes, bell pepper, zucchini, and red onion with olive oil, dried oregano, dried basil, salt, and pepper.
    - Spread the vegetables in a single layer and roast for 20-25 minutes, or until tender and slightly caramelized.
3. **Prepare the Dressing (Optional):**
    - In a small bowl, whisk together olive oil, lemon juice, Dijon mustard, honey or maple syrup, salt, and pepper.
4. **Assemble the Bowl:**
    - In bowls, layer the cooked quinoa with the roasted vegetables.
    - Drizzle with the optional dressing if using.
    - Add desired toppings like fresh herbs, feta or goat cheese, and sliced avocado.
5. **Serve:**
    - Serve immediately or store in airtight containers for meal prep.

This bowl is versatile—feel free to swap in your favorite vegetables or add protein like chickpeas or grilled chicken. Enjoy!

Pesto Chicken and Veggie Skewers

Ingredients:

- **For the Skewers:**
    - 1 lb (450g) chicken breast, cut into 1-inch cubes
    - 1 red bell pepper, cut into chunks
    - 1 zucchini, sliced into rounds
    - 1 small red onion, cut into chunks
    - 8-10 cherry tomatoes
    - 1/4 cup pesto (store-bought or homemade)
- **For Marinade (Optional):**

- 2 tablespoons olive oil
- 1 tablespoon lemon juice
- Salt and pepper to taste

Instructions:

1. **Marinate the Chicken (Optional):**
   - In a bowl, mix olive oil, lemon juice, salt, and pepper.
   - Add chicken cubes and toss to coat. Marinate for at least 15 minutes, or up to 1 hour in the refrigerator.
2. **Prepare the Skewers:**
   - Preheat your grill or oven to medium-high heat (about 400°F or 200°C).
   - Thread the chicken, bell pepper, zucchini, red onion, and cherry tomatoes onto skewers, alternating the ingredients.
3. **Add Pesto:**
   - Brush or spoon pesto over the skewers, coating the chicken and veggies evenly.
4. **Grill or Bake:**
   - **Grilling:** Place the skewers on the grill and cook for about 10-15 minutes, turning occasionally, until the chicken is fully cooked and has nice grill marks.
   - **Baking:** Arrange the skewers on a baking sheet and bake for about 20-25 minutes, turning halfway through, until the chicken is cooked through.
5. **Serve:**
   - Serve the skewers hot, garnished with extra pesto or fresh basil if desired. These are great with a side of rice, quinoa, or a fresh salad.

Enjoy these pesto chicken and veggie skewers as a delicious and easy meal, perfect for any occasion!

Creamy Avocado Pasta

Ingredients:

- 12 oz (340g) pasta (like spaghetti, fettuccine, or penne)
- 2 ripe avocados
- 2 cloves garlic
- 1/4 cup fresh basil leaves (plus extra for garnish)
- 2 tablespoons lemon juice
- 1/4 cup grated Parmesan cheese (or nutritional yeast for a vegan option)
- 1/4 cup olive oil
- Salt and pepper to taste

- Red pepper flakes (optional, for a bit of heat)

Instructions:

1. **Cook the Pasta:**
   - Cook the pasta according to package instructions. Drain and set aside, reserving 1/2 cup of pasta water.
2. **Prepare the Avocado Sauce:**
   - In a food processor or blender, combine avocados, garlic, basil, lemon juice, and Parmesan cheese. Blend until smooth.
   - With the blender running, slowly add olive oil until the mixture is creamy and well combined.
   - Season with salt and pepper to taste. If the sauce is too thick, add a bit of the reserved pasta water until it reaches your desired consistency.
3. **Combine:**
   - Toss the cooked pasta with the avocado sauce, adding more reserved pasta water if needed to help coat the pasta evenly.
4. **Serve:**
   - Garnish with extra basil, red pepper flakes (if using), and additional Parmesan cheese if desired.
   - Serve immediately and enjoy!

This dish is perfect for a quick weeknight dinner or a light lunch.

Stuffed Zucchini Boats

Ingredients:

- **For the Zucchini Boats:**
   - 4 medium zucchini
   - 1 tablespoon olive oil
   - Salt and pepper to taste
- **For the Filling:**
   - 1/2 lb (225g) ground turkey, beef, or sausage (or use a plant-based alternative)
   - 1 small onion, finely chopped
   - 2 cloves garlic, minced
   - 1 cup cherry tomatoes, diced (or 1 cup regular tomatoes, diced)
   - 1/2 cup cooked quinoa or rice (optional, for added texture)
   - 1 teaspoon dried oregano
   - 1 teaspoon dried basil
   - 1/2 teaspoon paprika
   - 1/2 cup shredded cheese (such as mozzarella, cheddar, or Parmesan)
   - Fresh herbs for garnish (like basil or parsley, optional)

Instructions:

1. **Prepare the Zucchini:**
    - Preheat your oven to 375°F (190°C).
    - Cut the zucchini in half lengthwise and scoop out the center with a spoon to create boats. Leave about 1/4-inch of zucchini flesh around the edges.
    - Brush the inside of the zucchini boats with olive oil and season with salt and pepper.
    - Place the zucchini boats cut-side up on a baking sheet.
2. **Prepare the Filling:**
    - In a skillet, heat 1 tablespoon of olive oil over medium heat.
    - Add the chopped onion and cook until translucent, about 3-4 minutes.
    - Add the minced garlic and cook for an additional 30 seconds until fragrant.
    - Add the ground meat (or plant-based alternative) and cook until browned and cooked through. Break it up with a spoon as it cooks.
    - Stir in the diced tomatoes, cooked quinoa or rice (if using), oregano, basil, and paprika. Cook for an additional 5 minutes, until the mixture is heated through and the flavors are combined.
    - Taste and adjust seasoning with salt and pepper if needed.
3. **Stuff the Zucchini:**
    - Spoon the filling into the prepared zucchini boats, packing it in tightly.
    - Sprinkle shredded cheese on top of each stuffed zucchini boat.
4. **Bake:**
    - Bake in the preheated oven for 20-25 minutes, or until the zucchini is tender and the cheese is melted and bubbly.
5. **Serve:**
    - Garnish with fresh herbs if desired.
    - Serve warm, either as a main dish or a side.

Feel free to customize the filling with other ingredients you enjoy, such as mushrooms, spinach, or different types of cheese. Enjoy your stuffed zucchini boats!

Lemon Garlic Shrimp with Spinach

Ingredients:

- 1 lb (450g) large shrimp, peeled and deveined
- 2 tablespoons olive oil
- 4 cloves garlic, minced
- 1 lemon, juiced (plus lemon zest for garnish)
- 1/2 teaspoon red pepper flakes (optional, for heat)
- 4 cups fresh spinach
- Salt and pepper to taste

- Fresh parsley, chopped (for garnish)

Instructions:

1. **Cook the Shrimp:**
     - Heat olive oil in a large skillet over medium-high heat.
     - Add minced garlic and cook for about 30 seconds until fragrant, being careful not to burn it.
     - Add the shrimp to the skillet in a single layer. Cook for 2-3 minutes on each side, until they turn pink and opaque.
2. **Add Flavor:**
     - Squeeze lemon juice over the shrimp and sprinkle with red pepper flakes if using. Stir to coat the shrimp evenly.
3. **Add Spinach:**
     - Add the fresh spinach to the skillet. Cook for 1-2 minutes, stirring, until the spinach wilts.
4. **Season and Serve:**
     - Season with salt and pepper to taste.
     - Garnish with lemon zest and chopped parsley.

This dish is great on its own or served over rice, pasta, or with a side of crusty bread. Enjoy your lemon garlic shrimp with spinach!

Beef and Sweet Potato Hash

Ingredients:

- 1 lb (450g) ground beef
- 2 large sweet potatoes, peeled and diced
- 1 small onion, diced
- 1 bell pepper (any color), diced
- 2 cloves garlic, minced
- 1 teaspoon smoked paprika
- 1/2 teaspoon ground cumin

- 1/2 teaspoon dried thyme or oregano
- Salt and pepper to taste
- 2 tablespoons olive oil or vegetable oil
- Fresh parsley or cilantro for garnish (optional)
- 1-2 tablespoons Worcestershire sauce (optional, for extra flavor)

Instructions:

1. **Prepare the Sweet Potatoes:**
   - In a large skillet or cast iron pan, heat 1 tablespoon of oil over medium heat.
   - Add the diced sweet potatoes and cook, stirring occasionally, until they start to soften and get golden, about 10-15 minutes. You may need to cover the pan to help the potatoes cook through.
2. **Cook the Beef:**
   - While the sweet potatoes are cooking, in a separate pan, heat the remaining tablespoon of oil over medium-high heat.
   - Add the ground beef and cook until browned, breaking it up with a spoon as it cooks. Drain any excess fat if needed.
3. **Combine Ingredients:**
   - Add the diced onion and bell pepper to the pan with the beef. Cook for about 5 minutes until the vegetables are softened.
   - Stir in the minced garlic, smoked paprika, cumin, and dried thyme or oregano. Cook for another 1-2 minutes until fragrant.
   - Add the cooked beef mixture to the skillet with the sweet potatoes. Stir well to combine.
4. **Season and Finish:**
   - Season the hash with salt and pepper to taste.
   - Stir in Worcestershire sauce if using for extra depth of flavor.
   - Cook for an additional 5 minutes, stirring occasionally, until everything is well combined and the sweet potatoes are fully cooked.
5. **Serve:**
   - Garnish with fresh parsley or cilantro if desired.
   - Serve hot, either on its own or with a side of eggs (fried or poached), avocado slices, or a dollop of sour cream.

Enjoy this savory and satisfying hash! It's a great way to enjoy a mix of flavors and textures in one delicious dish.

Moroccan Spiced Chickpeas

Ingredients:

- 1 can (15 oz) chickpeas, drained and rinsed (or 1.5 cups cooked chickpeas)
- 2 tablespoons olive oil
- 1 teaspoon ground cumin
- 1 teaspoon ground coriander
- 1 teaspoon smoked paprika
- 1/2 teaspoon ground turmeric
- 1/2 teaspoon ground cinnamon
- 1/4 teaspoon cayenne pepper (optional, for heat)

- 3 cloves garlic, minced
- 1 tablespoon lemon juice
- Salt and pepper to taste
- Fresh cilantro or parsley for garnish (optional)

Instructions:

1. **Prepare the Chickpeas:**
   - If using canned chickpeas, drain and rinse them well. Pat dry with a paper towel to remove excess moisture.
2. **Cook the Spices:**
   - Heat olive oil in a large skillet over medium heat.
   - Add the minced garlic and cook for about 30 seconds until fragrant, being careful not to burn it.
   - Add the cumin, coriander, smoked paprika, turmeric, cinnamon, and cayenne pepper (if using). Stir and cook for another 30 seconds to toast the spices.
3. **Add Chickpeas:**
   - Add the chickpeas to the skillet. Stir well to coat them with the spices.
   - Cook, stirring occasionally, for about 5-7 minutes, until the chickpeas are heated through and slightly crispy.
4. **Finish and Serve:**
   - Stir in the lemon juice and season with salt and pepper to taste.
   - Garnish with chopped fresh cilantro or parsley if desired.

Serving Suggestions:

- **As a Side:** Serve as a side dish with grilled meats or roasted vegetables.
- **In a Salad:** Toss into a salad for added protein and flavor.
- **In a Wrap:** Add to wraps or pita pockets with some greens and yogurt or tahini sauce.
- **With Rice:** Serve over rice or couscous for a complete meal.

Enjoy these Moroccan spiced chickpeas for a burst of exotic flavor and a healthy boost!

Baked Tilapia with Sweet Potatoes

Ingredients:

- **For the Tilapia:**
  - 4 tilapia fillets (about 6 oz each)
  - 2 tablespoons olive oil
  - 1 teaspoon paprika
  - 1 teaspoon garlic powder
  - 1/2 teaspoon onion powder
  - 1/2 teaspoon dried thyme or oregano

- Salt and pepper to taste
- Lemon wedges for serving (optional)
- **For the Sweet Potatoes:**
  - 2 large sweet potatoes, peeled and cubed
  - 2 tablespoons olive oil
  - 1 teaspoon smoked paprika
  - 1/2 teaspoon ground cumin
  - 1/2 teaspoon garlic powder
  - Salt and pepper to taste

Instructions:

1. **Preheat Oven:**
   - Preheat your oven to 400°F (200°C).
2. **Prepare Sweet Potatoes:**
   - Toss the cubed sweet potatoes with olive oil, smoked paprika, cumin, garlic powder, salt, and pepper.
   - Spread the sweet potatoes in a single layer on a baking sheet.
   - Bake for 20 minutes.
3. **Prepare Tilapia:**
   - While the sweet potatoes are baking, prepare the tilapia. In a small bowl, mix olive oil, paprika, garlic powder, onion powder, dried thyme, salt, and pepper.
   - Brush or rub the mixture evenly over the tilapia fillets.
4. **Add Tilapia to Oven:**
   - After the sweet potatoes have been baking for 20 minutes, remove the baking sheet from the oven.
   - Place the tilapia fillets on the baking sheet, alongside the sweet potatoes.
   - Return to the oven and bake for an additional 15-20 minutes, or until the tilapia is cooked through and flakes easily with a fork, and the sweet potatoes are tender.
5. **Serve:**
   - Serve the tilapia fillets with the roasted sweet potatoes.
   - Garnish with lemon wedges if desired.

Enjoy this balanced and flavorful meal that's easy to prepare and perfect for any night of the week!

Lentil and Sweet Potato Shepherd's Pie

Ingredients:

- 1 cup dried lentils (or 2 cups cooked)
- 1 large sweet potato, peeled and cubed
- 1 onion, chopped
- 2 garlic cloves, minced
- 2 carrots, diced
- 1 celery stalk, diced

- 1 cup vegetable broth
- 1 tablespoon tomato paste
- 1 teaspoon dried thyme
- 1 teaspoon dried rosemary
- Salt and pepper to taste
- Olive oil for sautéing

Instructions:

1. Cook lentils according to package instructions if using dried.
2. Boil sweet potato cubes in salted water until tender, then mash with a bit of olive oil, salt, and pepper.
3. In a skillet, heat olive oil and sauté onion, garlic, carrots, and celery until softened.
4. Stir in tomato paste, thyme, and rosemary, then add cooked lentils and vegetable broth. Simmer until thickened. Season with salt and pepper.
5. Preheat oven to 375°F (190°C).
6. Transfer the lentil mixture to a baking dish and top with mashed sweet potatoes, spreading evenly.
7. Bake for 25-30 minutes, or until the top is slightly golden.

Enjoy your meal!

Roasted Brussels Sprouts with Garlic and Lemon

Ingredients:

- 1 lb Brussels sprouts, trimmed and halved
- 3 cloves garlic, minced
- 2 tablespoons olive oil
- Zest and juice of 1 lemon
- Salt and pepper to taste
- Optional: red pepper flakes for heat

Instructions:

1. Preheat your oven to 400°F (200°C).
2. Toss Brussels sprouts with olive oil, garlic, salt, and pepper.
3. Spread them in a single layer on a baking sheet.
4. Roast for 20-25 minutes, stirring halfway through, until they're crispy and golden.
5. Remove from the oven, and toss with lemon zest and juice. Add red pepper flakes if desired.

Enjoy the zesty crunch!

Sweet Potato and Black Bean Enchiladas

Ingredients:

For the Enchiladas:

- 2 large sweet potatoes, peeled and cubed
- 1 tablespoon olive oil

- 1 teaspoon ground cumin
- 1 teaspoon smoked paprika
- 1/2 teaspoon garlic powder
- 1/2 teaspoon onion powder
- Salt and pepper to taste
- 1 can (15 oz) black beans, drained and rinsed
- 1 cup corn kernels (fresh, frozen, or canned)
- 1/2 cup chopped fresh cilantro
- 2 cups shredded cheese (cheddar, Monterey Jack, or a blend)
- 8-10 corn or flour tortillas

For the Enchilada Sauce:

- 1 tablespoon olive oil
- 1 small onion, chopped
- 2 cloves garlic, minced
- 1 can (15 oz) tomato sauce
- 1 cup vegetable broth
- 2 tablespoons chili powder
- 1 teaspoon ground cumin
- 1/2 teaspoon smoked paprika
- Salt and pepper to taste

Instructions:

1. **Prepare the Sweet Potatoes:**
    - Preheat your oven to 425°F (220°C).
    - Toss the sweet potato cubes with olive oil, ground cumin, smoked paprika, garlic powder, onion powder, salt, and pepper.
    - Spread them in a single layer on a baking sheet and roast for 20-25 minutes, or until tender and slightly caramelized. Set aside.
2. **Prepare the Enchilada Sauce:**
    - In a saucepan, heat olive oil over medium heat.
    - Add chopped onion and cook until softened, about 5 minutes.
    - Add minced garlic and cook for another minute.
    - Stir in tomato sauce, vegetable broth, chili powder, ground cumin, smoked paprika, salt, and pepper.
    - Simmer for 10 minutes, allowing the flavors to meld. Adjust seasoning as needed.
3. **Assemble the Enchiladas:**
    - Reduce the oven temperature to 375°F (190°C).
    - In a large bowl, combine roasted sweet potatoes, black beans, corn, and chopped cilantro.
    - Pour a thin layer of enchilada sauce into the bottom of a baking dish.

- Fill each tortilla with the sweet potato mixture and roll them up. Place seam-side down in the baking dish.
- Pour the remaining enchilada sauce over the top of the rolled tortillas and sprinkle with shredded cheese.

4. **Bake:**
   - Bake for 20-25 minutes, or until the cheese is melted and bubbly and the sauce is heated through.

5. **Serve:**
   - Let the enchiladas cool for a few minutes before serving. Garnish with additional cilantro, avocado slices, or a squeeze of lime if desired.

Enjoy your flavorful and hearty enchiladas!

Chicken and Mushroom Stir-Fry

Ingredients:

- 1 lb chicken breast or thighs, thinly sliced
- 2 cups mushrooms, sliced (button, cremini, or shiitake)

- 1 bell pepper, sliced
- 1 onion, sliced
- 2 tablespoons vegetable oil
- 3 cloves garlic, minced
- 1 tablespoon fresh ginger, minced
- 1/4 cup soy sauce
- 2 tablespoons oyster sauce (optional)
- 1 tablespoon hoisin sauce (optional)
- 1 teaspoon sesame oil
- 1 tablespoon cornstarch mixed with 2 tablespoons water (for thickening)
- Cooked rice or noodles for serving

Instructions:

1. **Prepare the Sauce:**
   - In a small bowl, mix soy sauce, oyster sauce, hoisin sauce, and sesame oil. Set aside.
2. **Cook the Chicken:**
   - Heat vegetable oil in a large skillet or wok over medium-high heat.
   - Add sliced chicken and cook until browned and cooked through, about 5-7 minutes. Remove from the skillet and set aside.
3. **Stir-Fry Vegetables:**
   - In the same skillet, add a bit more oil if needed.
   - Sauté garlic and ginger until fragrant, about 1 minute.
   - Add onions and bell pepper, cooking for 2-3 minutes.
   - Add mushrooms and continue cooking until tender, about 5 minutes.
4. **Combine and Finish:**
   - Return the chicken to the skillet.
   - Pour the sauce over the mixture and stir well.
   - Add the cornstarch mixture and cook until the sauce thickens, about 2 minutes.
5. **Serve:**
   - Serve hot over cooked rice or noodles.

Enjoy your savory and satisfying stir-fry!

Mediterranean Stuffed Eggplant

Ingredients:

- 2 large eggplants
- 1 tablespoon olive oil
- 1 onion, chopped
- 2 cloves garlic, minced
- 1 red bell pepper, diced
- 1 cup cherry tomatoes, halved

- 1/2 cup cooked quinoa or couscous
- 1/4 cup Kalamata olives, sliced
- 1/4 cup feta cheese, crumbled
- 2 tablespoons fresh parsley, chopped
- 1 teaspoon dried oregano
- Salt and pepper to taste

Instructions:

1. **Prepare the Eggplants:**
    - Preheat your oven to 375°F (190°C).
    - Cut the eggplants in half lengthwise and scoop out the flesh, leaving a 1/2-inch border. Brush the eggplant halves with olive oil and place them cut-side down on a baking sheet. Bake for 20 minutes.
2. **Make the Filling:**
    - Heat olive oil in a skillet over medium heat.
    - Sauté onion and garlic until softened, about 5 minutes.
    - Add red bell pepper and cook for another 3 minutes.
    - Stir in cherry tomatoes and cook until they start to soften, about 5 minutes.
    - Mix in the eggplant flesh, quinoa or couscous, olives, feta, parsley, and oregano. Season with salt and pepper.
3. **Stuff and Bake:**
    - Turn the eggplant halves cut-side up. Spoon the filling into each half.
    - Return to the oven and bake for an additional 20 minutes, until the eggplant is tender and the filling is heated through.
4. **Serve:**
    - Garnish with extra parsley and a drizzle of olive oil if desired.

Enjoy your Mediterranean-flavored dish!

Teriyaki Tofu and Vegetable Stir-Fry

Ingredients:

For the Stir-Fry:

- 1 block (14 oz) extra-firm tofu, drained and cubed
- 2 tablespoons vegetable oil (for frying tofu)
- 2 cups broccoli florets
- 1 red bell pepper, sliced
- 1 cup snap peas
- 1 large carrot, thinly sliced
- 1 onion, sliced
- 3 cloves garlic, minced
- 1 tablespoon fresh ginger, minced

For the Teriyaki Sauce:

- 1/4 cup soy sauce
- 2 tablespoons rice vinegar
- 2 tablespoons honey or maple syrup
- 1 tablespoon cornstarch mixed with 2 tablespoons water (for thickening)
- 1 tablespoon sesame oil
- 1 teaspoon grated fresh ginger
- 1 clove garlic, minced

Optional Garnishes:

- Sesame seeds
- Sliced green onions
- Chopped cilantro

Instructions:

1. **Prepare the Teriyaki Sauce:**
   - In a small bowl, combine soy sauce, rice vinegar, honey (or maple syrup), sesame oil, grated ginger, and minced garlic. Stir well.
   - In a separate bowl, mix cornstarch with water to create a slurry. Add this to the sauce mixture and whisk until smooth. Set aside.
2. **Cook the Tofu:**
   - Heat vegetable oil in a large skillet or wok over medium-high heat.
   - Add cubed tofu and cook, turning occasionally, until golden and crispy on all sides, about 7-10 minutes. Remove tofu from the skillet and set aside.
3. **Stir-Fry the Vegetables:**
   - In the same skillet, add a bit more oil if needed.
   - Add garlic and ginger, cooking for about 1 minute until fragrant.
   - Add onion, carrot, and broccoli. Stir-fry for 3-4 minutes.
   - Add bell pepper and snap peas, and continue to cook until vegetables are tender-crisp, about 2-3 more minutes.
4. **Combine and Finish:**
   - Return the cooked tofu to the skillet with the vegetables.

- Pour the teriyaki sauce over the tofu and vegetables. Stir well to coat everything evenly.
- Cook for an additional 2-3 minutes, or until the sauce has thickened and everything is heated through.

5. **Serve:**
    - Serve the stir-fry over rice or noodles.
    - Garnish with sesame seeds, sliced green onions, and chopped cilantro if desired.

Enjoy your flavorful and satisfying Teriyaki Tofu and Vegetable Stir-Fry!

Grilled Chicken with Roasted Red Pepper Sauce

Ingredients:

For the Chicken:

- 4 boneless, skinless chicken breasts
- 2 tablespoons olive oil
- 1 teaspoon paprika
- 1 teaspoon garlic powder
- 1 teaspoon onion powder
- Salt and pepper to taste

For the Roasted Red Pepper Sauce:

- 2 red bell peppers, roasted and peeled (or use jarred roasted red peppers)
- 2 cloves garlic
- 1 tablespoon olive oil
- 1 tablespoon balsamic vinegar
- 1/2 teaspoon dried basil
- 1/2 teaspoon dried oregano
- Salt and pepper to taste

Instructions:

1. **Prepare the Chicken:**
    - Preheat your grill to medium-high heat.
    - Brush chicken breasts with olive oil and season with paprika, garlic powder, onion powder, salt, and pepper.
    - Grill chicken for 6-7 minutes per side, or until the internal temperature reaches 165°F (74°C) and the juices run clear.
2. **Make the Roasted Red Pepper Sauce:**
    - If using fresh red bell peppers, roast them over an open flame or under a broiler until the skins are charred. Place them in a bowl covered with plastic wrap to steam, then peel off the skins.
    - In a blender or food processor, combine roasted red peppers, garlic, olive oil, balsamic vinegar, basil, oregano, salt, and pepper. Blend until smooth.
3. **Serve:**
    - Spoon the roasted red pepper sauce over the grilled chicken.
    - Garnish with fresh herbs if desired.

Enjoy your flavorful and vibrant meal!

Spaghetti Squash with Puttanesca Sauce

Ingredients:

For the Spaghetti Squash:

- 1 large spaghetti squash
- 1 tablespoon olive oil
- Salt and pepper to taste

For the Puttanesca Sauce:

- 2 tablespoons olive oil
- 3 cloves garlic, minced
- 1 can (14.5 oz) crushed tomatoes
- 1/4 cup Kalamata olives, sliced
- 2 tablespoons capers, rinsed
- 1/4 cup fresh parsley, chopped
- 1/2 teaspoon red pepper flakes (optional)
- 1 teaspoon dried oregano
- Salt and pepper to taste

Instructions:

1. **Prepare the Spaghetti Squash:**
   - Preheat your oven to 400°F (200°C).
   - Cut the spaghetti squash in half lengthwise and scoop out the seeds.
   - Brush the cut sides with olive oil and season with salt and pepper.
   - Place the squash cut-side down on a baking sheet and roast for 40-45 minutes, or until tender.
2. **Make the Puttanesca Sauce:**
   - While the squash is roasting, heat olive oil in a saucepan over medium heat.
   - Add garlic and cook until fragrant, about 1 minute.
   - Stir in crushed tomatoes, olives, capers, red pepper flakes (if using), oregano, salt, and pepper.
   - Simmer the sauce for 15-20 minutes, allowing the flavors to meld.
3. **Finish the Squash:**
   - Once the squash is roasted, use a fork to scrape out the strands into a bowl.
   - Toss the squash with a bit more olive oil if desired.
4. **Serve:**
   - Top the spaghetti squash with the puttanesca sauce.
   - Garnish with fresh parsley.

Enjoy your satisfying and healthy meal!

Creamy Coconut Curry with Cauliflower

Ingredients:

- 1 large head of cauliflower, cut into florets
- 1 tablespoon vegetable oil or coconut oil

- 1 onion, chopped
- 3 cloves garlic, minced
- 1 tablespoon fresh ginger, minced
- 2 tablespoons curry powder
- 1 teaspoon ground cumin
- 1/2 teaspoon turmeric
- 1 can (14 oz) coconut milk (full-fat for creaminess)
- 1 can (14 oz) diced tomatoes
- 1 tablespoon soy sauce or tamari
- 1 tablespoon brown sugar or maple syrup
- Salt and pepper to taste
- Fresh cilantro for garnish
- Cooked rice or naan for serving

Instructions:

1. **Roast the Cauliflower:**
   - Preheat your oven to 425°F (220°C).
   - Toss cauliflower florets with a little oil, salt, and pepper.
   - Spread on a baking sheet and roast for 20-25 minutes, or until tender and golden brown.
2. **Prepare the Curry Base:**
   - While the cauliflower roasts, heat oil in a large skillet or pot over medium heat.
   - Add chopped onion and cook until softened, about 5 minutes.
   - Add garlic and ginger, cooking for another 1-2 minutes until fragrant.
   - Stir in curry powder, ground cumin, and turmeric. Cook for another minute to toast the spices.
3. **Make the Sauce:**
   - Add coconut milk, diced tomatoes, soy sauce, and brown sugar to the skillet. Stir well to combine.
   - Bring to a simmer and cook for 10 minutes, allowing the sauce to thicken and flavors to meld.
4. **Combine and Serve:**
   - Add the roasted cauliflower to the sauce and stir gently to coat.
   - Simmer for an additional 5 minutes to heat through.
   - Season with salt and pepper to taste.
5. **Garnish and Enjoy:**
   - Garnish with fresh cilantro.
   - Serve hot over rice or with naan bread.

Enjoy your creamy and comforting coconut curry!

www.ingramcontent.com/pod-product-compliance
Lightning Source LLC
LaVergne TN
LVHW081612060526
838201LV00054B/2211